DARK
ENTRIES

WRITER
IAN RANKIN

ART
WERTHER DELL'EDERA

LETTERS
CLEM ROBINS

DARK
ENTRIES

DARK ENTRIES
VERTIGO CRIME

DARK ENTRIES Published by DC Comics, 1700 Broadway, New York, NY 10019. Copyright
© 2009 by DC Comics. All rights reserved. VERTIGO, VERTIGO CRIME and all characters,
the distinctive likenesses thereof and all related elements are trademarks of DC Comics.
The stories, characters and incidents mentioned in this book are entirely fictional.
DC Comics does not read or accept unsolicited submissions of ideas, stories or artwork.
Printed in Canada. First Printing. DC Comics, a Warner Bros. Entertainment Company.
HC ISBN: 978-1-4012-1184-4   SC ISBN: 978-1-4012-1386-2

Certified Chain of Custody
80% Certified Fiber Sourcing and
40% Post-Consumer Recycled
www.sfiprogram.org

NSF-SFICOC-C0001801
This label applies to the text stock

EARLY EVENING IN ANYTOWN...

ANYTOWN, ENGLAND.

TV CHEF'S PORN SHAME

I BUY A PAPER ON REFLEX.

NO NEWS INSIDE, JUST SYNAPSE-NUMBING JUNK.

SAME GOES FOR THE WHISKEY: REFLEX, THAT'S ALL.

THE TOP MODEL FELL FOR HIS ROCK STAR LOOKS...

NOT TO MENTION HIS MILLIONS.

SYNAPSE-NUMBING, TOO.

HIGLAND PARK ESTᵈ 1978
SINGLE MALT SCOTCH WHISKY
AGED 18 YEARS

"HIS HEAVY DRUG USE WAS NO BARRIER TO THEIR FIRST NIGHT OF PASSION."

IN A FIVE-STAR HOTEL SUITE.

YOU WOULD THOUGH, WOULDN'T YOU? IF HE ASKED?

BLOODY BUS. I'M GOING TO MISS "WORST CELEBRITY DRIVERS."

IT'S REPEATED LATER. EVERYTHING'S REPEATS THESE DAYS.

ANYTHING TO ERASE THE JABBER.

AN ENGLISHMAN'S HOME IS HIS CASTLE.

LOVE THY NEIGHBOR

F*CK U!

EVEN WHEN IT'S *NOT*.

DRAWBRIDGE DOWN, PORTCULLIS BREACHED.

DON'T MIND IF I SMOKE, DO YOU?

I STOPPED A FEW YEARS BACK, BUT LIKE WATCHING OTHERS DO IT. PUFF AWAY.

THANKS. BY THE WAY, DO YOU KNOW FRANCIS BACON?

HE WAS AN ARTIST. GUY BROKE INTO HIS STUDIO ONE NIGHT AND THE TWO ENDED UP BEST MATES. MIGHT *NOT* HAPPEN TO US.

I'M IN TELEVISION, MR. CONSTANTINE. THE COMPANY I WORK FOR PRODUCES SOME OF BRITAIN'S MOST WATCHED PROGRAMS.

OUR FIRST SUCCESS WAS WITH A *CHEF*, SADLY NOW OF SOME NOTORIETY.

NOW WE'VE GOT *"WORST CELEBRITY DRIVERS,"* WITH THE FORMAT SOLD TO A HUNDRED TERRITORIES WORLDWIDE.

WE KNOW WHAT WE'RE *DOING*, MR. CONSTANTINE.

I THINK I PREFERRED THE *SNOW.* SO IS THIS SOME NEW FORMAT YOU'RE TRYING OUT: *"NON-CELEBRITY BREAK-IN"*?

YOUR DOOR WASN'T LOCKED. I DIDN'T THINK YOU'D MIND A **CLIENT** MAKING HIMSELF AT HOME.

IS THIS WHERE YOU OFFER ME A GUEST SLOT ON "BRITAIN'S MOST HAUNTED"?

THAT'S NOT SUCH A BAD **GUESS**, MR. CONSTANTINE...

"WE CALL IT 'DARK ENTRIES.' WE'RE CONFIDENT IT'S ANOTHER RATINGS SMASH.

"THE CENTRAL CONCEPT IS **FEAR** AND HOW WE COPE WITH IT. THIS, WE FEEL, GIVES THE SHOW AN EDUCATIONAL SLANT. A HOUSE, ITS FRONT DOOR LOCKFAST. ROOMS AND CORRIDORS ALMOST WITHOUT NUMBER."

"RUNNING WATER, A WORKING KITCHEN. HOT FOOD DELIVERED DAILY BY DUMB-WAITER. *NO* CONTACT WITH THE *OUTSIDE WORLD*."

"EVERYTHING MONITORED... ABSOLUTELY EVERYTHING."

SO IT'S YOUR BASIC *HAUNTED HOUSE* SCENARIO?

MORE LIKE AGATHA CHRISTIE; "AND THEN THERE WERE NONE." A *GAME* IS BEING PLAYED, MR. CONSTANTINE.

"THERE ARE CONTESTANTS. SIX OF THEM. YOUNG AND IMPRESSIONABLE, EACH ONE A STRANGER TO THE OTHERS. THEY HAVE BEEN CHOSEN WITH A CERTAIN AMOUNT OF CARE: DIFFERENT **PERSONALITIES**, DIFFERENT **STRENGTHS**, DIFFERENT **WEAKNESSES**.

"**WE** CONTROL THE HOUSE, MR. CONSTANTINE.

"IT HAS BEEN DESIGNED WITH **ONE** THING IN MIND.

"FEAR."

"BUT THERE ARE CONSOLATIONS, TOO. AND ONE *BIG* PRIZE..."

"...LOTS OF SECRET TUNNELS AND ROOMS TO BE FOUND, LOTS OF EXPLORING FOR THE *BRAVE* AND THE *AMBITIOUS.*"

"AND BEHIND ONE DOOR AND ONE DOOR *ONLY*..."

"...AN *EXTRAORDINARY* PRIZE, AWAITING THE WINNER."

THANKS, I'LL BE SURE TO *TUNE OUT.*

FOR THE *FEE* I'M PREPARED TO OFFER, MR. CONSTANTINE, I HOPE YOU'LL MANAGE TO BE MORE POSITIVE.

YOUR REPUTATION IS NOT QUITE THE *SECRET* YOU THINK IT.

I'VE HEARD YOU CALLED A *"PARANORMAL INVESTIGATOR."* A NUMBER OF INDEPENDENT PRODUCERS HAVE EVEN PITCHED IDEAS TO ME ABOUT YOU WITHOUT YOU EVER BEING AWARE OF IT. BUT NOTHING FELT QUITE RIGHT...UNTIL *NOW.*

YOU WANT ME TO HELP YOU SCARE A BUNCH OF FAME-HUNGRY *KIDS?*

18

NOT AT ALL: WE'RE QUITE ABLE TO DO THAT ON OUR OWN. THE PROBLEM IS, I LIED TO YOU EARLIER. I SAID *WE* CONTROL THE HOUSE...

WE *DON'T.*

THE HOUSE... THE "SET"... SEEMS TO HAVE DEVELOPED A *MIND OF ITS OWN.*

THAT'LL BE GOOD FOR THE RATINGS.

ABSOLUTELY, BUT ALL THE SAME...

WHAT?

I'D VALUE YOUR ADVICE. ADVERTISERS WOULDN'T LIKE IT IF SOMETHING WENT WRONG.

WHAT COULD *POSSIBLY* GO WRONG...?

This morning I saw the burning man again.

BUT IS IT REALLY MORNING? NO WAY OF KNOWING. NO WINDOWS TO LOOK OUT OF. NO SUNSHINE, NO SOUNDS OF RAIN. WE SLEEP WHEN WE'RE TIRED, DAY OR NIGHT.

HE NEVER CRIES OUT. ONLY EVER SHOWS HIMSELF TO ME.

I THINK HE'S THE SCARIEST, BUT THEN I'M THE ONLY ONE WHO SEES HIM.

ISHMAEL'S THE OLDEST HERE; THINKS HE HAS TO BE BRAVE ON OUR BEHALF.

BUT THE GHOST CAR SCARES HIM. WHEN HE TALKS ABOUT IT, I SEE THE FEAR IN HIS EYES.

ALICE IS IN A WORLD OF HER OWN. SAYS THERE'S A BIG BIRD, KEEPS SWOOPING DOWN ON HER, BEAK SHARP AS A RAZOR.

THE SCARS ON HER ARMS WEREN'T CARVED BY ANY BEAK...

TOLD HER I'D SWAP FOR MY BURNING MAN ANY DAY.

I LIKE JUDE.
THERE'S THAT
WHIFF OF DANGER
ABOUT HIM. HE'S
FROM LONDON,
SAME AS ALICE.

HE WON'T TELL US
WHAT'S HAUNTING
HIM, BUT WE KNOW
THERE'S SOMETHING.
HE SEEMS MORE
EMBARRASSED
THAN SCARED.

WHEN JUDE
HEARD I'M FROM
NOTTINGHAM HE
KEPT WINDING
ME UP, TELLING
ME FOREST ARE
CRAP. HE'S A
CHELSEA FAN.
PROBABLY A
HOOLIGAN.

HE'S JUST LOOKING
FOR A REACTION, STEPH.
DON'T GIVE HIM THE
SATISFACTION.

THEY ALL CALL ME STEPH RATHER THAN **STEPHANIE**. ISHMAEL SAYS HE USED TO VISIT NOTTINGHAM ON BUSINESS. HE LOOKS AT ME FUNNY SOMETIMES.

HE THINKS MAYBE WE'VE MET BEFORE.

I KNOW WHAT HE MEANS.

SAME WITH JUDE AND ALICE. STRANGERS, BUT NOT QUITE.

AKIKO CAME OVER HERE FROM TOKYO. SHE DOESN'T SAY MUCH. STILL SPEAKS BETTER ENGLISH THAN JUDE.

WHEN SHE TOLD US ABOUT THE NEEDLES, JUDE JOKED THAT SHE WAS A JUNKIE.

WAY SHE JUST SITS THERE FOR HOURS, MAYBE SHE IS.

DOESN'T SEEM TO BOTHER TOM. HE TALKS TO HER CONSTANTLY, WHETHER SHE'S LISTENING OR NOT.

TOM'S A YANK, ALL THE WAY FROM SEATTLE. PACIFIC NORTHWEST, HE SAYS. MISSES HIS COMPUTER MORE THAN HIS LOVED ONES.

THE OLD WOMAN ISN'T ANYONE HE KNOWS.

SHE'S JUST THERE TO SCARE THE SHIT OUT OF HIM.

THEY WANT TO SCARE US OFF, THEY'VE GOT TO TRY HARDER.

TOO RIGHT.

HEAR THAT, VIEWERS?

WANT TO SEE US *SHITTING* OURSELVES, YOU'RE GOING TO HAVE TO RATCHET IT UP!

BUT THE BIRD, IT SEEMS SO REAL...COULD THEY BE MESSING WITH OUR HEADS?

YOU MEAN DRUGS?

WE EAT AND DRINK, DON'T WE?

WE CERTAINLY DO.

BE EASY FOR THEM TO TAMPER WITH IT.

NOT ENOUGH FOR MY LIKING. THIS STUFF'S WEAK AS *PISS*.

NOW HEAR THIS, ENGLAND! WE. ARE. *NOT*. FUCKING. SCARED!!

BUT WE ARE. SOME OF US ARE *PETRIFIED*. WE WANT OUT, AND THAT MEANS FINDING THE SECRET ROOM.

IT MEANS FINDING A WAY IN.

CLUES LEADING US THERE.

PAST ANY TRAPS, DODGING PITFALLS.

KNOWING WHO WE CAN TRUST.

IT'S QUITE A SETUP, MATTY.

I LIKE TO THINK SO.

AND PUNTERS ACTUALLY *WANT* TO BE STUCK IN THERE?

BECOMING CELEBRITIES IN THE PROCESS. WATCHED BY MILLIONS.

AND THE HANGAR HERE, IT'S NOT BUILT ON THE SITE OF A CEMETERY OR SOMETHING?

AUTHORISED PERSONS ONLY

YOU'RE THINKING OF THE FILM "POLTERGEIST"?

IF YOU'D SAID "YES," I COULD'VE COLLECTED MY CASH AND HOOFED IT.

I FEAR IT MAY NOT BE QUITE THAT SIMPLE. HOW ARE THE DARLINGS, BIANCA?

BEHAVING THEMSELVES. YOU MUST BE THE EXORCIST.

MAX VON SYDOW, AT YOUR SERVICE.

MAYBE IF WE SHOW MR. CONSTANTINE SOME OF THE FOOTAGE...?

ALL SET.

ISHMAEL THINKS THERE'S A CAR, RACING TOWARDS HIM.

AKIKO'S SEEING NEEDLES, STICKING UP FROM THE FLOOR.

AND HER?

STEPHANIE. IF SHE CLOSES HER EYES, THE BURNING MAN CAN'T GET HER.

AND *NONE* OF THIS IS YOUR DOING?

WE WEREN'T DUE TO START SCARING THEM UNTIL TONIGHT. FIRST WEEK IN THE HOUSE IS FOR ACCLIMATIZATION. THEN THEY STARTED SEEING THINGS, TALKING ABOUT IT.

SO BRING THEM OUT.

BUT THE RATINGS ARE *DYNAMITE!* AND NOW YOU'RE HERE...

MASS PSYCHOSIS...TEEN HYSTERIA...THEY'RE GIVING YOU JUST WHAT YOU ASKED OF THEM.

YOU'RE SAYING WE DO NOTHING? JUST LEAVE THEM TO FESTER?

NO NEED TO SOUND SO *ENTHUSIASTIC.*

THERE'S STUFF I COULD DO: SOME RITES, A FEW SPELLS AND INCANTATIONS. MIGHT CLEAR THE AIR A BIT. AND IF NOT, WE'LL TRY FENG SHUI.

I TOLD YOU THIS WAS A MISTAKE! THE MAN'S A COMPLETE FRAUD!

YOU SCARE KIDS FOR A LIVING... ANY CHANCE SOMEONE ON THE SHOW HAS THEIR OWN AGENDA?

OUR STAFF HAVE BEEN VETTED AND THE MANSION'S SECURE.

SHE REMINDS ME OF SOMEONE...

I THOUGHT SHE WAS YOUR TYPE, SAW IT STRAIGHT AWAY.

AND WHAT TYPE'S THAT THEN, LOVE?

THE DAMSEL IN DISTRESS.

SHOW ME THE TAPES AGAIN, AND ANY MORE YOU'VE GOT LIKE THEM. I'M ASSUMING YOU PSYCH-TESTED THE POOR SODS BEFORE LOCKING THEM UP: I WOULDN'T MIND SEEING THAT STUFF, TOO.

THEY WEREN'T CRAZY WHEN WE PUT THEM INSIDE, MR. CONSTANTINE.

DOESN'T MEAN THEY'RE NOT CRAZY NOW, MATTY, AND I'LL NEED BIANCA TO DO SOMETHING FOR ME.

WHAT?

MUG OF YOUR STRONGEST ROSIE-LEA, MILK AND TWO SUGARS.

AND IT'S NO GOOD SAYING I'M SWEET ENOUGH ALREADY...

WHY WOULD ANYONE WATCH THIS?

3:00

MAKING VOYEURS OF US ALL.

3:45

4:25

REMINDS ME OF BEDLAM. NINETEENTH CENTURY, THE GENTRY WOULD TAKE A SUNDAY PROMENADE AROUND THE INSANE ASYLUM.

IT GAVE THEM A BUZZ.

4:50

THIS LOT VOLUNTEERED, OF COURSE. DOESN'T MAKE IT ANY BETTER.

5:25

DOESN'T MEAN THEY'RE NOT BEING GOT AT.

5:50

DOESN'T MEAN THERE ISN'T SOMEONE PULLING THE STRINGS.

YOU CAN DO AMAZING THINGS WITH *CGI* THESE DAYS.

IF IT WERE *CGI*, WE'D BE ABLE TO SEE WHAT THE CONTESTANTS SEE.

UNLESS SOMEONE'S TAMPERED WITH THE CAMERAS. CHEERS, LOVE.

ANY *PROGRESS*, MR. CONSTANTINE?

SHE'S AN ICE MAIDEN, THAWING MAY TAKE A WHILE.

I MEANT WITH THE--

ONLY THING YOU CAN DO IS SHUT THE GAME DOWN, GO IN THERE YOURSELF AND CHECK THE PLACE OUT. DRINK WHAT THEY DRINK, EAT WHAT THEY EAT. WAIT TO SEE IF *YOU* GET THE WILLIES.

BUT IF WE *CAN'T* SHUT THE GAME DOWN...?

TELL ME YOU'RE NOT THINKING WHAT I *KNOW* YOU'RE THINKING.

AND AFTER YOU'VE DONE THAT, MAYBE YOU CAN LET *ME* IN ON THE SECRET, TOO.

IT'LL MEAN A BIGGER *FEE*, OF COURSE. YOU MAY EVEN BE THE ONE TO FIND THE *TREASURE*...

THE VIEWERS WILL LOVE IT: A SURPRISE *NEW CONTESTANT* ENTERS THE HAUNTED MANSION.

"LADIES AND GENTLEMEN: *JOHN* FROM *LIVERPOOL!*"

TEN...NINE...
EIGHT...

JOHN FROM LIVERPOOL, THAT'S ME. STILL TIME TO BACK *OUT*, THOUGH...

CAN'T EVEN TAKE MY BLOODY *CIGGIES* WITH ME: BLOODY GOVERNMENT BLOODY RULES. THINGS COULD GET MESSY, EVEN WITH AN ADDICT'S SUPPLY OF NICOTINE PATCHES.

SEVEN... SIX...FIVE...

FOUR... THREE... TWO...

MY SUITCASE HAS ALREADY GONE IN: ENOUGH FOR A COUPLE OF DAYS. DOESN'T MEAN I CAN'T BACK OUT. HAND KEENE BACK HIS CASH AND THE EXTRA CHEQUE...THE CHEQUE WITH ALL THOSE LOVELY *ZEROES*...

TOP OF THE WORLD, MA.

ACTION!

HE'S GOING IN NOW! BOY, ARE THE HOUSEMATES IN FOR A TREAT! JOHN, A FUN-LOVING SCOUSER WHO WORKS AS A MUSIC PROMOTER...

MUSIC PROMOTER WAS MY IDEA...NOT SO SURE NOW.

NOT SURE ABOUT *ANY* OF THIS, EXCEPT ONE THING.

THE GIRL CALLED STEPHANIE... SPITTING IMAGE OF *HELEN CAWDOR.*

NOT HER, OF COURSE, JUST *LOOKS* LIKE HER...

THING IS, I WAS TOO LATE TO *SAVE* HELEN. MAYBE THE BIG GUY'S GIVING ME ANOTHER CHANCE...

GOOD TO SEE A NEW FACE, MATE.

JUST THAT I WAS HOPING FOR A *BIRD,* NO OFFENSE.

GOOD NEWS IS, STEPHANIE'S HEAD'S STILL ATTACHED TO HER *NECK...*

TOLD YOU I COULD DO IT. HE WENT IN OF HIS OWN FREE WILL. *AND* SIGNED THE WAIVER.

SO NOW THE FUN *REALLY* BEGINS...

WHAT IS YOUR OCCUPATION, MR. CONSTANTINE?

IT'S *JOHN*. AND I'M IN THE MUSIC BIZ.

INTERESTING.

SHE COULD ALMOST BE RELATED... HELEN'S *COUSIN* MAYBE...

NOT REALLY. I PUT ON GIGS AND CLUB NIGHTS. NORTHEAST MOSTLY, NOWHERE YOU'D KNOW. SEEM TO *KNOW* YOU FROM SOMEWHERE THOUGH.

THAT TENDS TO HAPPEN IN HERE. SAME WITH ME AND ISHMAEL, JUDE AND ALICE...

IT'S LIKE WE'RE *CONNECTED* IN SOME WAY.

WE'RE THE *CHOSEN*, STEPH. AND WHEN WE GET OUT OF HERE, WIN OR LOSE, WE'LL BE THE BIGGEST BLOODY CELEBS IN *BRITAIN!*

IF NO ONE DIES OF *FRIGHT* FIRST.

YEAH, THERE MIGHT BE A SCARE OR TWO, BUT THE SHOW'S NOT GOING TO LET ANYTHING HAPPEN TO US. WE'D SUE THEIR *ARSES* OFF.

DO YOU EVER GET USED TO BEING WATCHED ALL THE TIME?

WE LIVE IN *BRITAIN*, JOHN. MORE C.C.T.V. ON THE STREETS THAN ANY OTHER COUNTRY IN THE WORLD.

AKIKO DOESN'T SOUND BRITISH.

MY HOME IS TOKYO.

SO HOW DID YOU FIND OUT ABOUT THE SHOW? READ ABOUT IT ON THE WEB?

YES... IT MUST BE SO.

AND THE REST OF YOU?

WHAT'S WITH THE QUESTIONS, NOSY BOY? YOU TRYING TO PSYCH US OUT? MAYBE YOU *ARE* A FUCKING MOLE!

JUST CURIOUS.

HELL HAPPENED?

FUSE, MAYBE.

THERE'S A TORCH IN ONE OF THE DRAWERS.

YOUR FIRST SHOT BETTER *KILL* ME, GEEK BOY.

ENOUGH, TOM. GO FIND AKIKO.

IN THE DARK?

SO MUCH FOR MACHO MAN. SCARED OF HIS OWN *SHADOW*.

LOOK WHAT I'VE FOUND...

ANYONE GOT A LIGHT?

USE ONE OF THE COOKER'S RINGS.

WE'LL GO IN GROUPS OF TWO, BE QUICKER FINDING HER.

LONG AS I'M NOT WITH *FRANK BRUNO* HERE.

YOU CAN GO WITH ALICE. TOM, YOU'RE WITH ME.

THOUGHT YOU AND ISHMAEL WERE SUPPOSED TO HAVE THIS "CONNECTION."

DOESN'T MEAN HE *LIKES* ME.

MIGHT AS WELL MAKE OURSELVES COMFORTABLE.

WHAT ABOUT AKIKO?

YOU GO IF YOU WANT. ME, I'M HAPPY WHERE I AM. THOSE LIGHTS WENT OUT FOR A *REASON.*

WHAT REASON?

THE FUSEBOX IS *FAKE,* NO WIRES GOING IN OR OUT. POWER IN THIS PLACE IS CONTROLLED FROM OUTSIDE. DON'T TELL ME YOU'VE FORGOTTEN THE *GAME* WE'RE PLAYING HERE?

STILL, GIVES US THE CHANCE TO GET *ACQUAINTED.* YOUR HEALTH.

TINK

I HATE NEEDLES.

EVER SINCE MY FIRST INOCULATION. THE PUNCTURE WOUND WAS SLOW TO HEAL. INFECTION SET IN.

THERE WAS A SMELL OF DEATH IN MY BEDROOM AS THE FEVER TOOK HOLD.

WHENEVER I CLOSED MY EYES, I SAW COLORS. PURPLES AND REDS AND GREENS. GREEN LIKE THE SEA, RED LIKE A GEISHA'S LIPSTICK. ALL OF THIS I REMEMBER.

BUT NOT LAST WEEK, AND NOT THE WEEK BEFORE THAT. MAYBE ALICE IS RIGHT: WE'VE BEEN DRUGGED.

MR. CONSTANTINE ASKED EXACTLY THE RIGHT QUESTION: WHAT AM I *DOING* HERE?

'BOUT BLEEDIN' TIME.

I DON'T KNOW ENGLAND. DID I TELL MY PARENTS I WAS COMING?

I'M IN THE DARK ABOUT SO MANY THINGS...

KLIK
PHISSSSSH

?

OPEN SESAME!

YOU TRYING TO GET ME SOZZLED?

DUNNO... WOULD IT HELP MY CHANCES?

IN FRONT OF AN AUDIENCE OF *EIGHT MILLION*? GET REAL.

BUT WITH ME UNCONSCIOUS, YOU CAN GO EXPLORING, MAYBE FIND THE SECRET ROOM.

GOOD POINT. SOUNDS SOLID ENOUGH.

SO WHAT BRINGS *YOU* HERE, JOHN? THE FAME? THE TREASURE?

MAYBE THE *COMPANY*. HOW ABOUT YOU?

SOUNDS STUPID, BUT I'M NOT REALLY *SURE* NOW.

MUST'VE KNOWN AT THE AUDITION, THOUGH.

I...DON'T REALLY REMEMBER ANY OF IT. WHOLE THING'S BEEN A BIT OF A BLUR.

MUST'VE MET THE CREW, THOUGH. THE PRODUCER-- MATTHEW KEENE? AND HIS BALL-BUSTING ASSISTANT BIANCA?

WE TALK TO MR. KEENE.

YOU TALK TO HIM?

IN THE THRONE ROOM.

AND WHAT'S THAT WHEN IT'S AT HOME?

IT'S HOW WE COMMUNICATE. HAVEN'T YOU BEEN WATCHING THE SHOW?

NO SIGN OF HER.

...HELL ARE YOU UP TO?

JOHN'S PLAYING THE GAME, THAT'S ALL.

COULD BE WHAT AKIKO'S DOING, TOO. OFF ON THE HUNT WHILE WE WASTE TIME TRYING TO TRACK HER DOWN.

MAYBE WE SHOULD ASK OUR MASTERS WHAT'S GOING ON. THIS *THRONE ROOM*, ANYONE GOING TO SHOW ME WHERE IT IS?

DO WE TELL HIM NOW?

PUBLIC SAYS HE SHOULD FIND OUT THE HARD WAY...MEANING MORE FUN FOR *US*.

SO KEENE SUMMONS YOU, AND YOU TROOP ALONG HERE? AND NONE OF YOU MET HIM BEFORE YOU CAME IN, OR AT LEAST YOU DON'T REMEMBER MEETING HIM...

BECAUSE NONE OF YOU REMEMBERS THE AUDITION, OR APPLYING TO BE ON THE SHOW. INTERESTING...

AKIKO CAN'T EVEN REMEMBER COMING TO ENGLAND. TO BE HONEST, SHE'S NOT THE **ONLY** ONE...

I CAN'T HELP THINKING THAT SOMEBODY SOMEWHERE IS HAVING A LAUGH. ONE WAY TO FIND OUT...

LET US IN, YOU CONNIVING BASTARDS!

ONE CONTESTANT **ONLY** AT A TIME IN THE THRONE-ROOM.

GOT TO BE **ME** THEN, EH?

PROMISE YOU'LL ASK ABOUT **AKIKO.**

TOP OF MY LIST, MATE.

WELL, **SECOND** TOP MAYBE...

ANY CHANCE THE CONDEMNED MAN CAN HAVE A *CIGGIE*?

WHAT MAKES YOU THINK YOU'RE CONDEMNED?

FIGURE OF SPEECH, THAT'S ALL. WHAT MAKES YOU ASK?

YOUR *FANS* ARE INTERESTED. THEY WANT TO KNOW WHAT MAKES YOU TICK.

I'VE HARDLY BEEN HERE FIVE MINUTES.

OUR VIEWERS HAVE *TAKEN* TO YOU, MR. CONSTANTINE.

THAT RIGHT? WELL, THEY CAN SHOVE IT UP THEIR JACKSIES. I'M *OUT*, KEENE.

OUT, MR. CONSTANTINE? THERE *IS* NO OUT, EXCEPT FOR THE SECRET ROOM.

THAT WHERE AKIKO IS?

POPULARITY

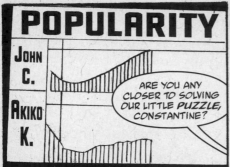

JOHN C.

AKIKO K.

ARE YOU ANY CLOSER TO SOLVING OUR LITTLE *PUZZLE,* CONSTANTINE?

THESE KIDS AREN'T HERE OF THEIR OWN FREE WILL--THAT MUCH I *DO* KNOW. THEY'VE NO IDEA HOW THEY GOT HERE OR WHAT THE HELL'S HAPPENING TO THEM. NOW TELL ME WHERE I CAN FIND AKIKO!

YOU SEEM TO BE GROWING CLOSER TO STEPHANIE. COULD SHE BE YOUR *SOUL-MATE?* TELL US HOW YOU'RE FEELING RIGHT NOW.

KNOW WHAT, KEENE? I CAN'T REALLY PUT IT INTO *WORDS.*

SO *THIS'LL* HAVE TO DO.

POPULARITY

JOHN C.

HE'S OFF THE SCALE.

HE CERTAINLY IS.

WE COULD BRING HIM BACK DOWN TO EARTH WITH A BUMP.

INTERESTING *PHRASE*, UNDER THE CIRCUMSTANCES...

HOUSE CONT

POINT MADE, I RECKON.

I'M SUPPOSED TO BE THE SHOW'S BAD BOY, JOHN. YOU KEEP *THAT* UP AND I'LL BE AFTER A NEW IDENTITY.

FUNNY YOU SHOULD SAY THAT, JUDE-- *IDENTITY'S* THE VERY THING WE NEED TO TALK ABOUT.

POWWOW IN THE REC ROOM?

AND SOME BEER TO WASH DOWN THE BUBBLY.

THEY DIDN'T SAY ANYTHING ABOUT AKIKO?

SORRY, TOM, NOTHING USEFUL. LISTEN, KEENE HAD ME SIGN LOTS OF FORMS BEFORE I CAME IN--ANY OF YOU REMEMBER THE SAME?

MY MIND'S A BLANK.

THAT'S WHAT WORRIES ME, STEPH. TIME TO GET IT OFF YOUR CHESTS.

WHAT?

THE VISIONS... THE THINGS IN HERE THAT ARE FREAKING YOU OUT.

I THOUGHT YOU HAVEN'T BEEN WATCHING THE SHOW.

I NEED YOU LOT TO TRUST ME.

SORRY?

A BIT LIKE THE CONFESSIONAL. I NEED TO HEAR EACH STORY IN TURN.

I STILL DON'T GET IT.

ME NEITHER, BUT I'M GOING TO TAKE JOHN AT HIS WORD. WHAT HAVE WE GOT TO LOSE?

MAYBE NOTHING. IT'S WHAT *HE* COULD GAIN THAT WORRIES ME.

FUCK IT. I'M OUTTA HERE!

HE'LL COME ROUND, DON'T WORRY.

MAYBE ONE OF US SHOULD GO AFTER HIM...

SCARED HE'S GOING TO BEAT YOU TO THE LOCKED ROOM, TOM?

HOW CAN I TELL THEM?

TELL THEM I'M SCARED OF AN OLD WOMAN'S *HANDBAG*?

I KNOW IT'S AN OLD WOMAN'S BECAUSE OF THE SMELLS--TALCUM POWDER AND VIOLETS. THOSE HEAVY SCENTS THEY USE TO DISGUISE THE SMELL OF *WEE*.

SUCH A STUPID THING TO BE SCARED OF. MY GRAN WAS DEAD BEFORE I WAS BORN. NEVER KNEW MY DAD, SO IT WAS JUST THE ONE DEAD GRAN--MUM'S MUM. THEN MUM DID A RUNNER WHEN I WAS SIX.

CHILDREN'S HOME WASN'T TOO BAD. I'D DO A RUNNER EVERY FEW WEEKS, LIVE ON THE STREETS. STAFF DIDN'T SEEM TO MIND, AND THE KIDS LOVED THAT I BROUGHT BACK CIGS AND HOOCH AND SOMETIMES EVEN A BIT OF BLOW.

KNEW WHERE I **WAS** BACK THEN. NOT SO SURE NOW.

STEPH TOLD ME ABOUT THE BURNING MAN. TOLD ME OTHER STUFF, TOO. ALICE'S DREAMS ABOUT THE SWOOPING BIRD; AKIKO AND HER *NEEDLES*.

ISHMAEL KEEPS THINKING A CAR IS COMING FOR HIM. FOR TOM, IT'S SOME OLD DEAR WITH HOLLOWED-OUT EYES. NONE OF IT ENGINEERED BY KEENE, UNLESS THERE'S SOMETHING IN THE WATER.

THERE'S SOMETHING ABOUT STEPH, THOUGH. IT'S NOT JUST THAT SHE REMINDS ME OF HELEN CAWDOR. SHE'S GOT AN *AURA*. MAYBE THAT'S WHAT DREW ME IN HERE--HER SENSE OF *OTHERNESS*...

I *LIKE* HER.

DON'T LOOK DOWN.

STOP WALKING.

DON'T LOOK.

GORE ROAD FLATS TO BE DEMOLISHED

NO SIGN OF MISSING HELEN

DON'T GO IN THERE.

DON'T LISTEN.

DON'T DO IT.
DON'T DO IT.
DON'T DO IT.

NOW YOU'VE GONE AND DONE IT, BRIAN...

UHN

HELLO, JOHN.

YOU LOOK LIKE YOU'VE SEEN A GHOST.

SO TELL US THE STORY, JOHN.

NOT MUCH TO TELL. IT WAS SIX YEARS BACK, GUY I KNEW CALLED *BRIAN McARTHUR*.

ACTUALLY, IT WASN'T BRIAN I KNEW AS MUCH AS HIS *GIRLFRIEND...*

...*HELEN CAWDOR.* KNEW HER FROM WAY BACK. BUT THEN SHE MET BRIAN. HE WAS A HISTORIAN, DABBLED IN ARCHAEOLOGY-- MYTHS AND LEGENDS.

STARTED RESEARCHING SAWNEY BEAN.

WHO?

"HE LIVED IN THE SCOTTISH COUNTRYSIDE. COULDN'T MAKE MUCH OF A GO OF IT, WHICH MIGHT EXPLAIN WHY HE DID WHAT HE DID."

CANNIBALISM?

SO THE STORY GOES. FAR AS BRIAN WAS CONCERNED, THAT'S ALL IT *WAS*, THOUGH--A *STORY.*

78

"BRIAN RECKONED SAWNEY BEAN WAS A *LEGEND*, CONJURED UP AS A COMMENTARY ON THE HIGHLAND CLEARANCES.

"IT'S A HARSH LANDSCAPE. OWNERS RECKONED THEY'D MAKE MORE MONEY FROM SHEEP THAN FROM TENANTS. PEOPLE WERE TURFED OUT OF THEIR HOMES, LIVELIHOODS STRIPPED FROM THEM...

"A LOT OF THEM *STARVED*..."

HUNGER DOES STRANGE THINGS TO A MAN.

I'M STILL NOT SURE I UNDERSTAND...

BRIAN GREW OBSESSED. HELEN CALLED ME, SAID SHE WAS WORRIED ABOUT HIM. TOLD ME HE WAS *CHANGING.*

"STARTED EATING HIS STEAKS RARER AND RARER, AND THEN *RAW.* RAW BACON, SAUSAGE, LAMB, LIVER. A NEIGHBOR'S CAT WENT MISSING. SQUIRRELS IN THE GARDEN WITH BITS TORN FROM THEM..."

"PSYCHIATRIST COULDN'T FIND ANYTHING WRONG WITH HIM. HELEN RECKONED IT WENT *BEYOND* THAT, ANYWAY. HER THEORY WAS, SAWNEY HIMSELF HAD TAKEN POSSESSION. BRIAN WASN'T *BRIAN* ANY MORE..."

THE PAIR OF THEM WENT *AWOL.* I TRACKED BRIAN DOWN. HE'D *KILLED* HELEN...

"END OF STORY."

EXCEPT IT *ISN'T*, IS IT?

NOT QUITE, NO.

"HE FELL NINE STORIES. BLOCK WAS DUE FOR DEMOLITION, SO I DRAGGED HIM BACK *INSIDE*."

AND NOW YOU'VE DREAMED ABOUT HIM.

BUT WHEN I OPENED MY EYES, HE WAS STILL *THERE*. SAME AS YOUR BURNING MAN...

YOUR ONCOMING CAR...

YOUR BIG SWOOPING BIRD...

YOUR SPOOKY OLD WOMAN.

SO WHAT DOES IT ALL MEAN?

BRIAN McARTHUR IS **DEAD**. I WATCHED IT HAPPEN. WHATEVER'S GOING ON HERE, DEATH IS **PART** OF IT.

I NEED YOU THINKING ABOUT THAT. ALL THESE PHENOMENA, THEY **MEAN** SOMETHING TO YOU. THEY'RE **NOT** RANDOM.

SO TRY TO REMEMBER. TRY **HARD**.

WHILE **YOU** GO LOOK FOR THE **TREASURE**?

I JUST WANT **OUT** OF HERE, ALICE. I WANT **ALL** OF US OUT OF HERE BEFORE ANYTHING **ELSE** HAPPENS.

HE'S **BETTER** THAN I **EXPECTED**.

KEEP OUT WITH THE RED LIGHT

I'M GLAD YOU'RE WARMING TO HIM. AFTER ALL...HE'S GOING TO BE **WITH** US FOR A CONSIDERABLE TIME.

THE CANDLES ARE REAL. CANDLES BURN DOWN.

AND THEN THEY NEED TO BE REPLACED. MEANING PEOPLE *COME* HERE.

THEY *RE-LIGHT* THE CANDLES WHEN THEY BLOW OUT.

ALL I HAVE TO DO IS WAIT, AND THEN *FOLLOW.*

FOLLOW THEM OUT OF THE *RABBIT HOLE...*

HAH! THEY LEFT A TORCH HERE.

MEANS THEY'RE ON *MY* SIDE. MEANS I'M *GETTING* SOMEWHERE.

TUNNEL SEEMS TWICE THE LENGTH OF THE HOUSE. MUST BE MY IMAGINATION.

KKRTCHCK-KKSSTCHKK KRRCHCH

NEVER BEEN SCARED OF TIGHT SPOTS. STAFF AT THE CHILDREN'S HOME USED TO LOCK ME IN THE CUPBOARD.

NEVER GOT THE SATISFACTION OF HEARING *ME* BEG...HELL'S THAT *NOISE?*

KRRCHCH

SOUNDS LIKE THERE'S A GLITCH IN THE *MACHINERY*...OR...

KKRTCH

WHAT THE HELL IS *THAT?*

KSSTCH

KKRCH

SKKRCH

EEYAAH!

RESULT.

KEEP OUT WITH THE RED LIGH—

AND ONE OF OUR *OWN* EFFECTS, FOR A CHANGE...

ANY SIGN OF LITTLE AKIKO?

SHE'S SITTING IN THE DARK.

WELL, WE CAN'T HAVE **THAT**, CAN WE?

I REMEMBER THE TRAIN HOME FROM SCHOOL. THE **UNDERGROUND** TRAIN. SOMETIMES THE CARRIAGES WOULD BE PLUNGED INTO DARKNESS. AND THEN...

THE MEN IN THEIR BUSINESS SUITS, THE SALARY-MEN. GOOD AT THEIR BUSINESS, LITTLE WIVES WAITING FOR THEM AT HOME.

I PRAY THE
DARKNESS
DOESN'T
COME.

I LET THEM KNOW: KEEP YOUR FILTHY HANDS TO YOURSELVES!

BUT THEN THE LIGHTS GO OUT, AND THE *TOUCHING* BEGINS...

I KNOW WHAT THEY'RE THINKING...

I KNOW WHY THEY DO IT...

I KNOW WHAT TO *DO*...

I KNOW WHAT TO DO.

I EMBRACE THE DARKNESS.

I EMBRACE THE LIGHT...

INTERESTING...

AND NOT *OUR* DOING.

THE LIGHT IS OURS, BIANCA.

BUT *THAT'S* NOT WHAT SHE'S REACTING TO, IS IT?

I THINK SHE'S STARTING TO REMEMBER.

SHE'S GOOD FOR WEEKS YET.

NEVERTHELESS... SAY THERE'S SOMETHING IN THERE WE DON'T KNOW ABOUT, SOMETHING WE DIDN'T COUNT ON.

AN EMPATH? WELL, CONSTANTINE'S--

THIS ALL STARTED BEFORE HE CAME IN. MAYBE HE'S NOT THE ONLY ONE WITH A TOUCH OF OTHERNESS...

IT COULDN'T HAPPEN.

NOT UNLESS THERE'S A CONNECTION... A DEGREE OF SEPARATION. IT WOULD EXPLAIN CONSTANTINE'S FEAR OF SAWNEY BEAN.

JUDE'S ON THE MOVE AGAIN.

TAKES MORE THAN A *CHIMERA* TO FAZE GOOD OLD JUDE. HIS MARROW'S BEEN TOUGHENED BY ADVERSITY. TIME TO SWITCH OFF AKIKO'S LIGHTS AGAIN, I THINK.

YES, SIR.

WHERE'S *ISHMAEL* OFF TO?

WHALE-HUNTING PERHAPS. TIME TO GIVE HIM A FRIGHT?

I'M SURE THE VIEWERS WOULD LOVE IT.

THEN LET'S KEEP THEM WAITING.

KEENE... YOU *ARE* EVIL.

I'M DRAWN TO STEPH, BUT I CAN SEE WHY SHE'D PREFER JOHN. ALL MY LIFE, I'VE BEEN LOSING OUT TO GUYS LIKE HIM: SELF-CONFIDENT, CHARISMATIC, PLAIN BLOODY *COCKY*.

THE HOUSE I GREW UP IN HAD AN ATTIC. WE REACHED IT BY A LADDER. YOU TUGGED ON A ROPE AND THE LADDER CAME SLIDING DOWN. I USED TO TELL MILLIE, WATCH IT DOESN'T CHOP YOUR *HEAD* OFF.

MILLIE USED TO LET ME PLAY WITH HER, EVEN THOUGH I WAS FIVE YEARS OLDER THAN HER.

AKIKO, IS THAT *YOU?*

WE'D HAVE TEA PARTIES WITH HER TEDDY BEARS. SHE WAS MUMMY, I WAS DADDY. OR WE'D PLAY GAMES OF TAG AND LEAP-FROG AND HIDE AND SEEK...

JUDE? STOP MUCKING ABOUT.

BOO!

M-M-MILLIE? BUT YOU'RE...

I WAS HIDING, THAT'S ALL, AND NOW YOU'VE FOUND ME.

IT'S BEEN SUCH A LONG TIME...BUT YOU'RE JUST THE SAME. YOU'RE *EXACTLY* THE SAME.

DON'T CRY, ISHY. YOU'VE *FINISHED* ALL THE CRYING, REMEMBER?

JESUS, MILLIE, YOU DON'T KNOW THE *HALF* OF IT.

BUT I *DO*. I KNOW *ALL* OF IT.

STILL GOT *MR. SNUFF*, I SEE.

HE NEVER LEFT ME, ISHY. WHY DID EVERYONE *ELSE* GO AWAY?

I WAS WATCHING THE WRONG GIRL... I NEVER FORGAVE MYSELF FOR THAT, MILLIE...NEVER. HONEST TO GOD.

I KNOW THAT, ISHY. I'M SORRY IT WAS ALL SO BAD.

DO WE NEED TO HOLD *HANDS* OR ANYTHING?

IT'S NOT A BLOODY *SEANCE*. ALL WE'RE DOING IS *TALKING*. SO WHY DON'T YOU START.

ME?

HOW LONG HAVE YOU BEEN IN ENGLAND, TOM?

NOT LONG. YOU COULD SAY I'M IN TRANSIT.

TRANSIT TO WHERE?

JAPAN. TO *STUDY*.

WHAT'S YOUR FIELD, TOM?

I DON'T KNOW...MAYBE NOT TO STUDY... THEN, MAYBE A *VACATION*.

SO TELL ME WHAT YOU KNOW ABOUT JAPAN.

I KNOW WHAT I READ ON THE *WEB*.

ANY CHANCE YOU COULD KNOW *AKIKO* FROM THE WEB?

I'D NEVER MET HER TILL SHE WALKED INTO THIS HOUSE.

I DIDN'T SAY YOU'D *MET* HER...

PLENTY WAYS OF KNOWING SOMEONE WITHOUT MEETING THEM.

YOU MEAN LIKE *AVATARS*? ONLINE VERSIONS OF OURSELVES?

I DON'T USE COMPUTERS MUCH, PREFER TO GET MY INFORMATION THE *OLD FASHIONED* WAY...

TV?

NEWSPAPERS.

WHAT'S HAPPENING TO US, JOHN?

I THINK YOUR MINDS HAVE BEEN *WIPED*. NOT SURE WHY.

OUR MINDS...BUT NOT *YOURS*?

FAR AS I CAN TELL.

YOU'RE A *MOLE.*

GOT IT IN ONE.

NOT A *MUSIC PROMOTER?* CLUB NIGHTS IN THE NORTHEAST...?

BUT I DO A PRETTY MEAN '80s *MIX-TAPE*-- CURE, SMITHS, COCTEAUS.

I *KNEW* THERE WAS SOMETHING ABOUT YOU!

JUST TOO POLITE TO SAY, EH, TOM? I'D PROBABLY PUT SOME *DIRE STRAITS* ON *YOUR* TAPE...

"TEARS FOR FEARS...

"MADNESS..."

...AND ERASURE. WELCOME *BACK*, ISHMAEL.

WHERE'VE YOU *BEEN*? CONSTANTINE HERE IS A GODDAMNED *MOLE*. SAYS THAT FUCKER KEENE HAS WIPED OUR MEMORIES.

THEN HOW COME I REMEMBER MY *SISTER*?

HE MEANS *RECENT* MEMORIES-- HOW WE GOT HERE, WHY THE HELL WE VOLUNTEERED IN THE FIRST PLACE.

MAYBE WE *DIDN'T* VOLUNTEER. MAYBE WE WERE *DRUGGED*, SNATCHED FROM THE STREET.

NOT SURE *PRESS-GANGING'S* ACCEPTABLE THESE DAYS, EVEN FOR THE SAKE OF GOOD TELEVISION. ON THE *OTHER* HAND...

"I LOOKED IN STEPH'S ROOM. NO *CLOTHES*.

"I'M GUESSING IT'S THE SAME FOR *ALL* OF YOU. DON'T YOU FIND THAT A BIT *ODD?*"

MAYBE WE ALL SCREWED UP OUR LIVES SOMEWHERE AND THIS IS THE PUNISHMENT. THE PUNISHMENT...OR THE *CURE*.

THAT WOULD MAKE US *PRISONERS*.

WHAT MAKES YOU THINK WE'RE *NOT*?

CAN *YOU* HELP US, JOHN? IS THERE SOME *EMERGENCY EXIT* WE DON'T KNOW ABOUT?

THAT'S NOT A BAD IDEA! IF WE STARTED A FIRE OR SOMETHING, THEY'D *HAVE* TO SEND HELP.

EXCEPT...

SPRINKLERS.

FIRE EXTINGUISHERS.

NOT FORGETTING THAT THE SHOW'S DRIVEN BY *RATINGS*, AND SOMETHING TELLS ME OUR WONDERFUL VIEWERS WOULD *RELISH* THE CHANCE TO WATCH US DODGING THE FLAMES.

AND HOW CAN WE TRUST ANYTHING *YOU SAY*, YOU GODDAMNED *JUDAS*?

I'D SAY I'M THE *LEAST* OF YOUR BLOODY PROBLEMS RIGHT NOW!

JOHN'S RIGHT. THE WAY OUT OF HERE IS TO FIND WHAT CONNECTS US. FIGHTING AMONG OURSELVES IS JUST WHAT THEY *WANT*. THIS WHOLE GAME'S ABOUT SETTING US IN OPPOSITION TO EACH OTHER.

I WAS UPSTAIRS. THEY SHOWED ME MY *SISTER*. SHE SEEMED SO REAL, BUT I WAS JUST A KID WHEN SHE DIED.

WAS IT A *CAR ACCIDENT?*

HOW DID *YOU* KNOW?

YOU DREAM ABOUT HEADLIGHTS, A CAR COMING TOWARDS YOU. THESE NIGHTMARES, THEY'RE THINGS WE'RE AFRAID OF...THINGS FROM OUR *PAST*.

SO *TELL* ME, ALICE, JUST WHEN DID A HUGE *BIRD* SWOOP DOWN AND CARRY YOU OFF TO ITS *EYRIE?*

IT MIGHT *NOT* BE AN ACTUAL BIRD.

AN AIRPLANE MAYBE...

OR ANYTHING *SHARP*, ANYTHING THAT CAN *CUT*.

YES...MAYBE...

WHAT DO *YOU* THINK, JOHN?

I THINK I'D LIKE IT BETTER IF WE WEREN'T ALWAYS BEING *SPIED ON*.

SPIED ON BY *YOUR EMPLOYERS*, YOU MEAN.

WHY *DID* THEY SEND YOU IN HERE ANYWAY?

THE HOUSE IS SUPPOSED TO SCARE YOU, BUT NOT THE WAY IT'S BEEN *DOING*. KEENE AND HIS CREW WANT TO KNOW WHAT'S GOING ON.

THE DREAMS, THE NIGHTMARES... NOTHING TO DO WITH THE *SHOW*. THEY'D HAVE PULLED THE *PLUG*, BUT THE RATINGS HAVE BEEN *DYNAMITE*.

WELL, THAT'S *SOMETHING*, I SUPPOSE...

ON THE OUTSIDE, I'M A SORT OF *DETECTIVE*.

CRASHH

AND ON THE *INSIDE*, YOU'RE A NINE-STONE *WEAKLING*.

GOOD THAT YOU CAN KEEP A SENSE OF *HUMOR*, SWEETHEART.

WHAT MAKES YOU THINK THE ONLY CAMERAS THEY HAVE ARE THE ONES WE CAN *SEE*?

SOME KIND OF *BUG*. SOMETHING TELLS ME IT WON'T BE THE *ONLY* ONE.

IF YOU WERE REAL, I'D EAT YOU RAW. BETTER BE SOME BLOODY *FOOD* WAITING IN THIS SECRET BLOODY ROOM.

GOOD NEWS IS, THERE'S NOT ROOM IN HERE FOR HANDBAG CRAP TO START RAINING DOWN ON ME...

AW, HELL...

IT IS SIMPLE *COWARDICE*, AKIKO, WHICH DRAGS YOU FROM THE DARKNESS. THE SAME COWARDICE YOU SHOWED ON THE JOURNEY TO AND FROM SCHOOL.

NOT STANDING UP FOR *YOURSELF*, NOT TELLING THOSE MEN TO THEIR FACES THAT YOU THOUGHT THEM THE LOWEST FORM OF LIFE. GOING HOME AND PUTTING ON YOUR *DISGUISE*.

TRYING TO BE SOMEONE ELSE...*ANY-ONE* ELSE.

YOUR GRANDMOTHER DIED A DIABETIC. HER SYRINGE IS STILL IN THE BATHROOM, HEAVY AND METALLIC WITH A CLEAR GLASS BODY.

HEY, AKIKO!

FANCY MEETING *YOU* HERE...

PHISSH

WHAT CAN I DO FOR YOU, CONSTANTINE?

THOUGHT YOU'D WANT A *PROGRESS REPORT,* KEENE.

SO YOU *HAVE* MADE SOME *PROGRESS?*

I'VE DONE THE *SHERLOCK HOLMES* THING; COME TO A FEW *DEDUCTIONS.*

AND WHAT MIGHT **THOSE** BE?

I NEED A **CIGARETTE**, KEENE. SEND ONE IN AND I'LL TELL YOU WHAT I KNOW.

BIG OF YOU.

MY SIDE OF THE BARGAIN, CONSTANTINE.

WHEN YOU'VE ELIMINATED THE PROBABLE, WHATEVER'S *LEFT* HAS TO BE *TRUE.* LIKE MY THINKING, KEENE?

GO ON.

THEY'RE *DEAD,* AREN'T THEY? ALL SIX OF THEM--NOT *ONE* OF THEM'S ACTUALLY ALIVE.

TELL ME *WHY* YOU THINK THAT.

DON'T SHIT A SHITTER, KEENE.

HOW ARE YOU GOING TO BREAK THIS NEWS TO THEM? THEY'LL SAY YOU'RE *CRAZY.*

THERE'S A **BIGGER** QUESTION THAN THAT, KEENE. BECAUSE IF THEY'RE **DEAD**, THAT MEANS I'M **NOT** IN ANY REALITY FUCKING **TV** SHOW.

OH, BUT YOU **ARE!** ONE WE'VE BEEN WANTING YOU TO JOIN FOR SOME CONSIDERABLE TIME, ONLY WE COULDN'T THINK OF A WAY YOU'D **ACCEPT.**

BUT YOU **DID** ACCEPT... YOU SIGNED THE CONTRACT, AND THAT MAKES YOU **OURS** FOR THE **DURATION**...

YOU'RE OUR **STAR ATTRACTION**, CONSTANTINE. OUR VIEWERS ARE **BAYING** FOR YOU, **LITERALLY** BAYING.

SO WHAT **ELSE** DO YOUR DEDUCTIONS TELL YOU?

IF THE HOUSEMATES ARE THE **DEAR DEPARTED**, THAT MEANS I'M IN HEAVEN OR HELL. ANY POINT IN ME GUESSING **HEAVEN**?

NONE AT ALL, CONSTANTINE...

YOU SIGNED YOURSELF *OVER,* BODY AND SOUL. OTHER PLAYERS WILL COME AND GO, BUT NOT *YOU,* CONSTANTINE.

GOT YOU NOW, JOHN! BEEN VOTING FOR *YEARS* TO GET YOU DOWN HERE! COULDN'T BE FUCKING *HAPPIER,* YOU PRICK!

BRIAN? IS THAT *YOU?*

YOU *BET* IT'S ME--AND WHO WAS IT *PUT* ME HERE?

CANNIBALS DON'T GO TO HEAVEN, BRIAN.

123

ME TELLING THEM THEY'RE IN HELL, REDUCED TO PLAYTHINGS, PIECES IN A DEMON'S GAME. PROBABLY QUALIFIES AS "INTERESTING"...MIGHT EVEN STRETCH TO "MIND-BLOWING."

LAST THING I WANT IS PEOPLE AROUND ME WITH BLOWN MINDS. MAKES *SENSE* NOW, THOUGH...

BRIAN McARTHUR...*HE* MUST HAVE SEEN THE RESEMBLANCE, KNEW I'D BE *INTRIGUED*. KNEW IT MIGHT BE ENOUGH OF A SNARE.

STEPH, SPITTING IMAGE OF MY FRIEND *HELEN*, THE FRIEND I COULDN'T SAVE.

HOW DO I TELL THEM? *WHAT* DO I TELL THEM? WHEN? "HEY GUYS, ANYONE SMELL *CHARNEL* AROUND HERE?"

THE GENTLE TOUCH.

NEVER BEEN MY *STRONG SUIT*, DIPLOMACY...

BEDSIDE MANNER.

SO...WHY WIPE THEIR MEMORIES? TO MAKE THE GAME ALL THE *CRUELER* WHEN THEY FINALLY REALIZE THE *TRUTH?*

WALKED RIGHT INTO IT THOUGH, DIDN'T YOU? KNEW AT THE BACK OF YOUR MIND THERE WAS MORE TO IT, BUT THAT DIDN'T STOP YOU. COLD HARD CASH AND THE MEMORY OF NEVER QUITE GETTING TO SHAG HELEN CAWDOR, AND YOU'RE SIGNED UP FOR THE DURATION.

WAY *IN* MEANS THERE'S A WAY *OUT*. AND WHAT ABOUT THAT SECRET ROOM? IF IT REALLY EXISTS, WHAT'S *INSIDE*?

CHRIST, *LISTEN* TO YOU. WHAT'S THE POINT OF AN ESCAPE HATCH? ONLY THING WAITING OUT THERE IS HELL. HELL AND *BRIAN McARTHUR*.

HIM AND EVERY *OTHER* FUCKER I'VE SENT DOWN HERE.

PENNY FOR THEM.

HOW LONG'VE YOU BEEN THERE?

NOT LONG. SEEMS THE OTHERS HAVE *CRASHED*.

STEPH? WHAT *IS* IT?

NOTHING, JOHN. JUST... NOTHING.

IT'S COMING BACK, ISN'T IT? YOU'RE REMEMBERING WHAT *HAPPENED* TO YOU.

WHAT *DID* HAPPEN TO ME, JOHN? YOU'RE SO SMART, YOU TELL ME.

YOU'RE EVERY BIT AS SMART AS *I* AM, STEPH.

THE ONLY TIME I'VE REALLY FELT *ALIVE* SINCE WALKING IN HERE WAS WHEN WE MADE LOVE...

135

"I TRACKED HIM DOWN. HADN'T LAID EYES ON HIM IN FIVE OR SIX YEARS, BUT HE HADN'T *CHANGED*. DIDN'T SEEM SURPRISED WHEN I RANG THE BELL. LET ME IN, WHISKEY ON HIS BREATH...*THAT* HADN'T CHANGED, EITHER.

"HE USED TO...USED TO *DO* THINGS, TIL THE NIGHT MY MUM PLUCKED UP THE COURAGE TO GRAB ME AND RUN. I NEVER FORGAVE HIM. AND HERE HE WAS, LIVING THE HIGH LIFE WHILE WE GOT BY ON *HANDOUTS*.

"MUM TRIED GETTING MONEY OUT OF HIM, BUT HE ALWAYS HAD SOME EXCUSE. YET *HIS* PLACE WAS A *PALACE*.

"*BATHROOM* WAS THE SIZE OF THE PLACE ME AND MUM WERE *LIVING*."

YOU *ALL* ARE. AND SOMEHOW YOU'VE ENDED UP TRAPPED IN THIS DAMNED GAMESHOW--BY WHICH I MEAN A GAMESHOW SET UP TO AMUSE THE *DAMNED*. YOU'RE IN HELL, STEPH, WE ALL ARE. AND I'M THE ONLY ONE STILL *LIVING*.

WE'VE MANAGED TO EXPLAIN THE BURNING MAN, BUT THERE'S GOT TO BE SOME CONNECTION TO THE OTHERS. HANG ON, DIDN'T ISHMAEL SAY HE SOMETIMES WENT TO NOTTINGHAM?

AND HE KEEPS BEING HAUNTED BY AN ONCOMING CAR! STEPH, THAT'S *GOT* TO BE IT.

STEPH?

I'M DEAD?

DID YOU NOTICE HOW QUICK YOU JUMPED INTO *BED* WITH ME? YOUR BODY'D NOTED MY *LIFE FORCE*, AND IT *WANTED* SOME.

BUT RIGHT NOW WE HAVE TO CONCENTRATE ON *WHY* YOU'RE HERE. BECAUSE MY HUNCH IS, IF YOU WERE MEANT TO BE IN HELL IN THE FIRST PLACE, THEN THAT'S WHERE YOU'D BE.

I'VE NEVER FORGOTTEN MILLIE AND NEVER FORGIVEN MYSELF FOR WHAT HAPPENED.

"AND WHEN IT HAPPENED AGAIN, BUT THIS TIME WITH *ME* AS THE DRIVER... HISTORY REPEATING, JUST LIKE THE SONG SAYS. AND TOO MUCH TO BEAR.

"WHEN THEY TOLD ME...

"...TOLD ME I'D KILLED THE YOUNG WOMAN... THEY TRIED SAYING IT WASN'T MY FAULT...

BUT YOU *TOPPED* YOURSELF ANYWAY.

AKIKO, YOU AND TOM FELT A CONNECTION, BUT YOU LIVED IN TOKYO AND TOM IN SEATTLE. ARE THERE *ANY* CLUES YOU CAN GIVE US, ANYTHING AT *ALL*?

IT HAS BEEN RETURNING TO ME SLOWLY. I HAD ANOTHER SELF. MY OTHER SELF WROTE THINGS ON THE INTERNET...

A *BLOG*?

"I WROTE ABOUT MY DAYS IN TOKYO, MY FEELINGS, ALL SORTS OF THINGS. THERE WERE SITES I VISITED OFTEN. THEY WERE FOR PEOPLE LIKE ME.

"SOME OF THEM PROPOSED SUICIDE PACTS. WE WOULD SHOW THE WORLD OUR CONTEMPT. BUT I HAD *ANOTHER* PLAN.

"THERE WAS AN OLD SYRINGE IN MY PARENTS' BATHROOM, AND BOTTLES OF INSULIN. I PLANNED MY REVENGE."

"THE GUN WAS PLASTIC, CAME WITH A VIDEO GAME I'D GOTTEN TIRED OF.

"SHE WAS ALREADY DEAD. *HEART ATTACK* MAYBE.

"COPS TURNED UP SAME TIME AS THE PARA-MEDICS.

"I DON'T KNOW HOW MANY TIMES THEY *FIRED*..."

JUST LEAVES **YOU** TWO.

WHY IS IT I REMEMBER **NOW**? WHY WAS I BLOCKING IT BEFORE?

SO...IN YOUR OWN TIME...AND KEEPING THE **VOLUME** DOWN...

WASN'T **YOU** DOING THE BLOCKING, ALICE, LOVE.

"IT WAS IN THE PAPERS. THE WOMAN WHO'D KILLED HER ABUSIVE DAD... THE GUY WHO'D CRASHED INTO HER...WHO'S ALREADY SPENT MOST OF HIS LIFE GRIEVING FOR HIS SISTER. ALL SO SAD...SO SAD.

"LAST THING I BLOODY NEEDED, I CAN TELL YOU. STRAWS AND CAMELS' BACKS AND ALL THAT SHIT."

"EASY MEAT, THE CRUSTIES, EVEN WHEN THEY PUT UP A FIGHT. AND BY CHRIST, THIS ONE *DID*.

"SCREAMING FIT TO *BURST*. I KNEW MY TIME WAS RUNNING OUT.

"ALL I WANTED WAS THE CASH... ENOUGH FOR MY NEXT SCORE. FUNNY, I'D BEEN WONDERING WHY I HADN'T FELT THE NEED SINCE COMING IN HERE.

"SUPPOSE *DEATH* EXPLAINS IT AS WELL AS ANYTHING."

"LOOKED AROUND ME, NO ONE WATCHING. NEVER THOUGHT TO LOOK UP..."

LIKE THE PUNCHLINE TO A BAD JOKE.

SORRY ABOUT THAT, JUDE.

YOU *KILLED* ME, YOU FUCKER.

I READ YOUR STORY, ALICE! IT WAS ON THE SUICIDE WEBSITE!

TAMPERING WITH THE EYES IS FORBIDDEN. YOU WILL ALL BE PUNISHED!

AND HOW YOU GONNA DO THAT IF WE'RE ALREADY IN HELL?!

WAIT A MINUTE--WE'VE ONLY GOT YOUR WORD FOR IT THAT WE'RE ALL CORPSES AND YOU'RE NOT.

WHY WOULD I LIE?

A MILLION REASONS! WHAT MAKES YOU THINK YOU'RE STILL ALIVE? HOW CAN YOU EVEN BE HERE IF THAT'S THE TRUTH?

162

IF WE'RE ALREADY DEAD...

YES?

"THEN HOW CAN WE BE *KILLED?*"

FAR AS I UNDERSTAND IT, YOU *CAN'T.* DOESN'T MEAN YOU CAN'T BE MADE TO *SUFFER.*

I THINK YOU'RE WHAT'S KNOWN AS AN EMPATH. YOU STARTED THE CHAIN OF EVENTS, AND WHEN HELL BROUGHT YOU HERE AS A CONTESTANT, THE OTHERS IN THE CHAIN NATURALLY FOLLOWED.

BUT BROUGHT US FROM *WHERE*?

FROM LIMBO.

THE CHURCH SAYS LIMBO DOESN'T EXIST.

FAT LOT *THEY* KNOW.

IS EVERYTHING TO YOUR SATISFACTION, BIANCA?

OUR **MASTER'S** SATISFACTION IS WHAT'S PARAMOUNT. THE GAME IS FOR **HIS** PLEASURE, REMEMBER.

OH, I'M SURE **YOU'VE** BEEN PLEASURING OUR MASTER TO THE VERY **HILT.** BUT MAYBE IT'S TIME YOU **TOLD** HIM...

TOLD HIM **WHAT?**

THE MANSION HAS BEEN BREACHED. HELL HAS BROKEN IN. DON'T TELL ME YOU DON'T KNOW WHAT **THAT** MEANS...?

SPIT IT OUT, KEENE.

PRETTY SOON, **ALARM** BELLS ARE GOING TO START RINGING IN LIMBO.

THE GAME'S ALMOST UP, BIANCA.

184

DRAWBRIDGE *RAISED*, PORTCULLIS *CLOSED*...

CRAASHH

I WONDER IF THE OTHERS REACHED LIMBO. AND DO THE DEAD REALLY GIVE A SHIT WHERE THEY END UP?

I SHOULD FEEL BAD ABOUT *STEPH*, THOUGH. I KNOW I SHOULD. BUT SHE KILLED HER OLD MAN, AND THESE THINGS HAVE A WAY OF BALANCING OUT.

PAYBACK, YOU MIGHT CALL IT.

THEN AGAIN, MAYBE *NOT*.